TOOLS FOR CAREGIVERS

- **ATOS:** 0.6
- **GRL:** C
- **WORD COUNT:** 40

- **CURRICULUM CONNECTIONS:** colors, insects, nature

Skills to Teach

- **HIGH-FREQUENCY WORDS:** a, and, has, have, I, in, is, it, one, out, see, they, this, we, what
- **CONTENT WORDS:** away, black, blue, fly, nest, red, stay, stinger, wasps, wings, yellow
- **PUNCTUATION:** exclamation points, periods, question mark
- **WORD STUDY:** long /a/, spelled ay (away, stay); long /e/, spelled ee (see); long /i/, spelled y (fly); long /o/, spelled ow (yellow); /ow/, spelled ou (out)
- **TEXT TYPE:** information report

Before Reading Activities

- Read the title and give a simple statement of the main idea.
- Have students "walk" though the book and talk about what they see in the pictures.
- Introduce new vocabulary by having students predict the first letter and locate the word in the text.
- Discuss any unfamiliar concepts that are in the text.

After Reading Activities

Ask readers what they knew about wasps before reading this book. Have they ever seen one? What color was it? Re-read pages 14–15. Why do readers think they should stay away from wasps and their nests? Can they think of any other insects that can sting or bite?

Tadpole Books are published by Jump!, 5357 Penn Avenue South, Minneapolis, MN 55419, www.jumplibrary.com

Copyright ©2020 Jump!. International copyright reserved in all countries. No part of this book may be reproduced in any form without written permission from the publisher.

Editor: Jenna Trnka **Designer:** Michelle Sonnek

Photo Credits: efilippou/iStock, cover; Marco Uliana/Shutterstock, 1, 2tl, 10–11; Mircea Costina/Shutterstock, 2tr, 3; Shishka4/Shutterstock, 4–5; Brian Bevananthe/Pantheon/SuperStock, 2bl, 6–7; Ant Cooper/Shutterstock, 2br, 8–9; Nature PL/SuperStock, 2ml, 12–13, 16; Cristina Romera Palma/Shutterstock, 14–15.

Library of Congress Cataloging-in-Publication Data
Names: Nilsen, Genevieve, author.
Title: I see wasps / by Genevieve Nilsen.
Description: Tadpole books edition. | Minneapolis, MN: Jump!, Inc., (2020) | Series: Backyard bugs | Audience: Age 3–6. | Includes index.
Identifiers: LCCN 2018050522 (print) | LCCN 2018051944 (ebook) | ISBN 9781641288064 (ebook) | ISBN 9781641288040 (hardcover: alk. paper) | ISBN 9781641288057 (paperback)
Subjects: LCSH: Wasps—Juvenile literature.
Classification: LCC SB945.W3 (ebook) | LCC SB945.W3 N55 2020 (print) | DDC 595.79—dc23
LC record available at https://lccn.loc.gov/2018050522

I SEE WASPS

by Genevieve Nilsen

TABLE OF CONTENTS

tadpole
books

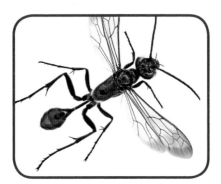

blue

nest

red

stinger

wings

yellow

I SEE WASPS

nest

I see a nest.

What is in it?

wasp

Wasps!

wing

They have wings.

They fly out.

yellow

This wasp is black and yellow.

This one is blue!

This one is red!

stinger

This one has a stinger.

We stay away!

15

LET'S REVIEW!

Not all wasps are black and yellow. They can be different colors! What color is this wasp?

INDEX